Adam and Eve are enjoying living peaceably with all the animals in the Garden of Eden.

God has told Abraham and his son Isaac to climb a mountain, taking plenty of firewood.

Jacob has gone to sleep in the desert. He is dreaming about angels climbing up and down from heaven.

Jacob has given his best-loved son Joseph a
wonderful new coat. His brothers are very jealous!

Moses is climbing down the mountain.
He is carrying stones with God's laws written on them.

David is fighting this giant, called Goliath.
David is hurling a stone at the giant. Who will win?

Here is Elijah. He's flying up to heaven in a chariot of fire!

Sailors have tossed Jonah out of their boat.
Where is he going to finish up?

These shepherds have come to see baby Jesus.
Do you know who told them where to find Jesus?

John is baptizing Jesus in the river.
A dove is flying over Jesus' head.

Jesus has just brought this little girl back to life.
It's a wonderful miracle!

This poor man can't walk, so friends have carried him to Jesus.
The house is so full they have let him down through the roof.

This boy left his home and family – and now he's come back.
How happy he's made his father!

This boy is giving Jesus his lunch – five loaves and two fish.
With this food, Jesus will feed more than 5,000 people!

Zacchaeus is very small, so he's climbed a tree
to make sure he has a good view when Jesus visits.

Jesus has risen from the dead. Mary is so very happy!